MW01167152

Fire TV User Guide:

The Ultimate Guide to Master Your Amazon Fire TV

Just got your hands on the Amazon Fire TV Streaming Device?

Learn what most owners of this new multimedia-streaming device DON'T...and transform this powerful device into your ultimate entertainment and gaming machine!

By
Daniel Forrester
Author & Tech Enthusiast

Table of Contents

Introducing Amazon Fire TV

Amazon Fire TV is a digital media player developed by Amazon and released on April 2, 2014. With Amazon Fire TV, you can stream movies, TV, music, and other digital media directly to your TV or monitor. The Amazon Fire TV is compatible with some of the most often used streaming platforms, including Netflix, Hulu, Pandora, ESPN, and Vevo.

Amazon Fire TV is designed to integrate easily into your preexisting home entertainment setup. It also syncs readily with your Amazon or Amazon Prime account, so that you can begin enjoying all the content the Amazon database has to offer within minutes.

With your Amazon Fire TV, you can also play exciting games and use amazing apps, all on your home TV screen.

Amazon Fire TV also features Amazon Voice Search, a new and innovative way to browse or quickly find the content you're searching for.

The device is operated via a slender remote with voice-control capabilities, or via the Amazon Fire Game Controller, which is sold separately.

What's In The Box?

Your Amazon Fire TV box should contain:

Amazon Fire TV (1)
This square-shaped unit connects to your TV or monitor via an HDMI cable.

Amazon 16W Power Adapter (1)
This connects to the back of the unit to power the Amazon Fire TV.

Amazon Fire TV Remote (1)
This voice-activated device operates your Amazon Fire TV unit.

Quick Start Guide (1)
A small sheet with quick start instructions for your Amazon Fire TV.

AAA Batteries (2)
These power your Amazon Fire TV Remote.

Amazon Fire TV Specifications

Amazon Fire TV	
Price	$99
Size (inches)	0.7 x 4.5 x 4.5
Wi-Fi	Dual Band
Ethernet	Yes
HDMI	Yes
Video Resolution	1080p
Optical Audio	Yes
Processor	1.7 GHz quad-core Qualcomm
Memory	2 GB
Screen Mirroring	Via Kindle Fire HDX
Remote	Yes
Voice Search	Yes
Game Controller	Yes ($39 Extra)
Netflix	Yes
Hulu Plus	Yes
HBO Go	No
Amazon Instant Video	Yes
Total Channels/Apps	100+

Operation

To begin using your Amazon Fire TV, plug the Amazon 16 W Power Adapter into the back of the unit. The unit should power on automatically; this will be indicated by a yellow light on the front of the device.

Next, connect your Amazon Fire TV via HDMI cable to your TV or monitor. The HDMI port is located on the back of the device, directly to the right of the power port. Connect your HDMI cable to the HDMI port, and connect the other end to your TV or monitor's HDMI In. Select the appropriate HDMI input on your TV. You should see the Amazon Fire TV startup screen.

To begin the digital setup, insert the included AAA batteries into your Amazon Fire Remote Control. Press the Play/Pause button, on the remote's lower row, to begin the setup process.

Connecting to the Internet

If you are using a hard-wired connection, also known as Ethernet, simply connect an Ethernet cable to the back of your Amazon Fire TV, in the appropriate port. The Ethernet port is the second port from the right, next to the USB port. Your device should automatically begin installing the required software.

If you prefer to use a wireless, or WiFi, connection, plug-in and connect the device to your TV as described in the steps above. Upon startup, the Fire will automatically detect available networks. Select your home network by scrolling to it and pressing Select, the large circular button in the middle of your remote control. If the network is password protected, you will be required to enter your password. If not, Fire will automatically logon.

Note: If your network is hidden, you will need to manually enter its information. To do so, scroll to the end of available networks, select "Join Other Network" and enter your network name and information.

About Amazon Accounts

To begin using your Amazon Fire TV, you must create an account with Amazon.com. If you already have an account, you can use your existing account to register with Amazon Fire TV.

Either way, you will need an Amazon account to start using Amazon Fire TV, as you will sync it with your Amazon Fire TV, and use it to purchase movies, TV shows, apps, and games. More information about using your Amazon account information with Amazon Fire TV is provided in the following pages, in the Registering Your Device section.

A basic Amazon account is free and easy to create. Simply navigate your web or mobile browser to amazon.com and find the "sign in" section on the main page (usually in the upper right-hand corner).

When you click "sign in" you will see an option to register as a "new customer." Select this option to begin the registration process. Registration is quick and easy, and furthermore, necessary for you to begin streaming content to your Amazon Fire TV.

Keep your amazon.com login information handy, as you will use the same credentials to begin using your Fire TV.

It is important to understand that your Amazon Fire TV draws media from two different Amazon-based sources, Amazon Instant and Amazon Prime. The content available to you via these two sources is different, depending on the source.

There are some other important differences between the account types, and it is useful to review these differences before deciding which service to use.

Amazon Instant Video

Amazon Instant Video products are available to anyone who has a basic Amazon account. These are movies and TV shows provided by Amazon for immediate streaming to any of your home media devices, including your personal computer, Amazon-compatible tablet device, or, most relevantly, your Amazon Fire TV.

These videos are accessed on a pay-per-view basis, meaning that you pay a flat fee to either rent or buy the title. Titles are available in both high definition (HD) and standard definition (SD). Please note that not all devices support high definition video, although your Amazon Fire TV does.

Amazon Instant Video rentals are generally about $10 less than Amazon Instant purchase prices, and expire after a set period of time. Once this time has elapsed, you will need to either purchase or rent the video again to view it. If you purchase media from Amazon Instant Video, you will be able to stream the video to any compatible device any time you so desire.

Amazon Prime

Amazon Prime is a membership program offered by Amazon that gives you free two-day shipping on most products, with no minimum order size required, access to instant streaming of over 41,000 moves and television episodes, as well as the ability to borrow eBooks free of charge from a selection of more than 350,000.

As opposed to Amazon Instant, Amazon Prime charges a flat fee of $79 annually, and gives you access to all the video content that is available on Amazon Prime, in addition to the other services mentioned above.

If you sign in with your basic Amazon account, you will not be able to access Amazon Prime content, but will still be able to access Amazon Instant movies on a pay-per-view basis.

If you are already an Amazon Prime customer, or have upgraded to Amazon Prime for the purposes of using your Amazon Fire TV, you will have automatic access to Amazon Prime content, without having to pay-per-view.

Please note, however, that some content is still exclusively available on Amazon Instant Video, and not necessarily free for Prime users. For some Amazon Instant content, you will still have to pay the rental or purchase price, even if you are an Amazon Prime user. When browsing Amazon's website or your Amazon Fire TV choices, you will see that there is some overlap between available content on Amazon Prime and Instant, but that this overlap is not by any means complete.

In subsequent sections, you will see mention to both Amazon Instant and Amazon Prime content. It is useful to keep these distinctions in mind while perusing this manual.

Amazon Cloud Drive

Amazon Cloud Drive is an online storage system that you can use to store your personal media, including videos, music, photos, and more. You do not have to have Amazon Cloud Drive installed to use your Amazon Fire TV, but it will enhance your experience significantly.

Some content, such as photos, can only be uploaded via your Amazon Cloud Drive, and so it is a necessary component of performing certain functions on your Amazon Fire TV.

Using Amazon Cloud Drive

Installing and using the Amazon Cloud Drive is quite simple. Please note, however, as mentioned above, you can also access your Amazon Cloud Drive from your personal computer or mobile smartphone. To transfer any content to your Cloud Drive that you would like to be available on Amazon Fire TV, you must transfer it via one of these means.

To install Amazon Cloud Drive on your computer, navigate to the Amazon main page, and type "cloud drive" into the search box. Downloads for Mac and PC are free and should be among the first results.

Alternatively, you can enter into your browser's URL bar:

For PC Computers - http://www.amazon.com/Amazon-Cloud-Drive-PC-Download/dp/B00FW6LGN2

For Mac Computers - http://www.amazon.com/Amazon-Cloud-Drive-Mac-Download/dp/B00FW6ME2O/

Downloads of Amazon Cloud Drive and related Cloud Drive products are free.

To install Cloud Drive for Android or iPhone smartphone devices, go to your device's native app store and search for "Amazon Cloud Drive".

Follow the steps for installation to begin using your Cloud Drive. Once your Cloud Drive is installed, you can upload your personal files, up to five gigabytes (5 GB) worth, for free. Files are saved in Amazon's online cloud and do not take up room on your computer or smartphone.

Please note that some features which Amazon Cloud Drive presents are not currently compatible with Amazon Fire TV, such as personal music streaming. While you can stream music through your Amazon Fire TV via Pandora or other music streaming apps, you cannot currently stream music you have uploaded to Amazon Cloud Drive.

The primary use of Amazon Cloud Drive, as of this writing, is to transfer photos and personal videos that can be viewed on your Amazon Fire TV. These can be viewed as a slideshow, or set as your Amazon Fire TV screensaver.

Photos on Amazon Cloud Drive

Uploading photos to Amazon Cloud Drive requires the additional installation of the Amazon Cloud Drive Photos app. As with the basic Cloud Drive app, this is available both for your personal computer and for your mobile smartphone.

As with the basic app, you can visit your mobile smartphone's app store to find the Amazon Cloud Drive Photo app. Once installed, photos uploaded to the app will be viewable on your Amazon Fire TV.

To install Amazon Cloud Drive Photos on your computer, please visit:
http://www.amazon.com/Amazon-Cloud-Drive-Photos-Storage/dp/B00A11AN6O

Registering Your Device

Once your Amazon Fire TV has connected to the Internet, either via Ethernet cable or WiFi, you will be prompted to register your device. To register your device, you will either need to login with your Amazon credentials, or create a new account.

If you already have an Amazon account, select "Register" on the left side of the screen. If you need to make a new account, select "Create an Account" from the right side.

When your device is successfully registered, using your username and password, the Amazon Fire introductory video will begin. This video showcases some of the main features of Amazon Fire TV and offers some introductory instruction to using your Amazon Fire TV.

Setting Up Your Amazon Fire TV

Immediately after the introductory video, you will be prompted to choose whether or not to enable parental controls. Parental controls require that a personal identification number (PIN) of your own devising is required to purchase and download any videos, apps, or in-app items. This measure ensures that no content will be downloaded or accessed that may be inappropriate for children.

To enable parental controls, select "Enable Parental Controls" using the select button on your Amazon Fire remote control. You will then be asked to enter a PIN. Make sure to keep this number in a safe place, as you will need it to download and access content.

After you've set up your PIN, you will be asked to specify in which situations you would like Amazon Fire TV to require your PIN. These include requiring a PIN for all purchases, requiring a PIN only for Amazon Instant Video, or requiring a PIN only to access or download certain types of content, e.g., games, apps, or photos.

After you set these controls you will proceed to the main screen.

If you would like to proceed without enabling parental controls, simply select "No Parental Controls." You will automatically proceed to the main screen.

Remote Control Basics

Microphone
Voice Search
Navigation
Select
Menu
Back
Home
Rewind
Play/Pause
Fast Forward

The Amazon Fire remote control is designed for efficiency and ease of use, and, as such, uses a limited number of controls to manipulate your Amazon Fire TV.

Microphone - The Amazon Fire remote has a small, built-in microphone that detects your voice when you perform a voice search. It is located directly above the voice search button.

Voice Search - Press this button to activate voice search functionality. This can be used to search for movies, TV shows, games, or apps. For more info, see Using Voice Search, below.

Navigation and Select Circle – The select circle is the large, grey circle in the center of your remote. You can use this to select an option, movie, TV show, game, or app from any of Amazon Fire TV's menus. It is surrounded by the black navigational circle.

Press up, down, right, or left on this circle to scroll through any menu.

Back – Returns to the previous screen.

Home – Returns to Amazon Fire's home screen from any screen.

Menu – Reveals menu information specific to whichever screen you are currently accessing.

Rewind – Scrolls backwards through playing media. Press the button once to jump back 10 seconds in time, or hold it down to continuously scroll backwards. Additional presses allow you to choose from various rewind times.

Play/Pause – Play or pause the current media. Press once to pause playing media, and then press gain to continue playing.

Fast Forward - Scrolls forwards through playing media. Press the button once to jump forward 10 seconds in time, or hold it down to continuously scroll forward. Additional presses allow you to choose from various fast forward times.

Using Voice Search

Using Amazon Fire TV's voice search function is a quick and easy way of skipping straight to your desired content.

To use the voice search function, hold the remote control 1 – 8 inches away from your mouth, with the microphone facing towards you. Press and hold the voice search button. The voice search prompt will appear onscreen, with the "listening" dialogue present. While you speak, level bars will indicate that the remote microphone is picking up your voice.

Wait until the tone sounds, then say the name of the movie, TV show, app, or game you would like to access. There is no need to issue directives such as "search" or "look up" into the microphone. Simply say the name of the content you would like to search.

For example, you could say "24" to search for the TV show, or "Netflix" to open the Netflix app.

Once you are done speaking, release the voice search button. In a few seconds, Amazon Fire TV will present you with text indicating what it "heard." If this text is correct, press the select button to view the search results. Your desired content will usually be the first result. Press the select button again to access the movie, TV show, game, or app.

Some notes on voice search:

- In addition to searching by titles of movies and TV shows, you can search by actor, director, or character names as well.

- Do not speak in full sentences, as Amazon Fire TV voice search is not programmed to interpret natural language. Instead, say only the name of the show, movie, game, or app you'd like to access.

- Try to ensure that background noise is minimal and that only one person attempts to use voice search at a time.

Amazon Fire Home Screen

The Amazon Fire Home screen is the main screen, which will start up whenever you turn on Amazon Fire TV. From this screen, you can depart to navigate any of Amazon Fire TV's sub-menus.

There are two distinct panes available from the Home screen. The first, running along the left side of your screen, presents the available categories of media, and search and settings options.

The right side of your screen presents thumbnail images showcasing some of the available media on your Amazon Fire TV. These include recently added titles and top titles for movies, TV, apps, and games. These categories show titles that have recently become available, or those which are the most popular among all Amazon Prime users.

There is also a recommended category, showing Amazon Prime's recommended TV and movies.

Your home screen also shows recent activity on your account, usually media which you have recently viewed. This is your personal Amazon Fire TV history. To show your recently viewed media, scroll up to "recent" and select this category. You will be taken to your recently viewed media.

By scrolling through the title thumbnails, you can choose to resume titles you have paused, add or remove titles from your watchlist (see Using the Watchlist, below), or remove titles from your Recent list. If you remove a title from your Recent list, it will no longer appear either from the home screen or within the Recent menu.

Different categories of media can be accessed from the left pane of your Home screen. Scroll to the left pane using the navigation circle, where you can scroll between options.

Search – Select this option to search media. From this menu, you can choose to search either via voice search, as detailed above, or text search. To text search, select the option, and begin to enter your search terms. Select letters with the select button and scroll to the next letter using the navigation circle. The list below will evolve to predict the your search terms as you fill in more detail.

Home – Return to the home screen.

Movies – Access your main movies menu. From here, you can view movies available on Amazon Prime, presented in different categories. These include new releases, top movies, and recommended movies, recommended by Amazon Fire TV based on your particular tastes. Movies are also searchable by genre, and presented as editor's picks, curated list based on thematic connections. You can also view your recently watched movies list within this menu.

TV – Access your main TV menu. From here, you can view TV shows available on Amazon Prime, presented in different categories. These include new releases, top TV, and recommended TV, recommended by Amazon Fire TV based on your particular tastes. TV shows are also searchable by genre, and presented as editor's picks, curated list based on thematic connections. You can also view your recently watched TV list within this menu.

Watchlist – Amazon Fire TV's Watchlist is a personally assembled collection of media which you bookmark for later viewing. If you have not yet added anything to the Watchlist, this menu will be empty.

Using the Watchlist - To add an item to the Watchlist, browse or search for TV or movies as you usually would. When you find a title you would like to add to the Watchlist, scroll to it. Beneath the movie or TV thumbnail, you should see options to either

"Watch Now" or "Add to Watchlist." Select "Add to Watchlist" and exit the menu (by either hitting the back or home buttons).

When you return to your Watchlist, you should now see the title. You can play this TV show or movie as you typically would. To remove a title from the Watchlist, scroll to that title within your Watchlist, and select "Remove from Watchlist," beneath the thumbnail.

Video Library – You can find your rented or purchased movies or TV shows in the video library. These are movies and shows that you purchase from within Amazon Prime, either online or via your Amazon Fire TV. Once purchased, these titles will reside in the video library. For more information on purchasing and renting video, please see Watching Movies and Watching TV, below.

Games – You can find your purchased games here. Games for purchase are also presented in popular lists, spotlights, and by categories. For more information on purchasing and playing games, please see Playing Games on Your Amazon Fire TV, below.

Apps - You can find your purchased and downloaded apps here, under your apps library. Apps are also presented in popular lists, spotlights, and by categories. For more information on buying, downloading, and using apps, please see Using Apps on Your Amazon Fire TV, below.

Photos – Here you can access photos and personal videos uploaded to the Amazon Cloud Drive. Media are presented as uploaded, either as individual photos or videos, or within albums. You can also add new photos and videos from this menu, via the Amazon Cloud Drive App. For more information on the Amazon Cloud Drive and adding photos, please see Using Amazon Cloud Drive above.

Settings – Access your main settings screen here. You can modify, among other things, account settings, parental controls, and system controls. For more information, please see Amazon Fire TV Settings, below.

Watching Media On Your Amazon Fire TV

Now that you've set up your Amazon Fire TV and familiarized yourself with the Home and menu screens, you are ready to start using it to watch movies and TV, play games and use a host of apps!

Watching Movies

Movie content can be accessed from the home screen one of two ways: either via the appropriate category in the left menu pane, or by scrolling through one of the thumbnail menus in the right pane of the main screen. Movie content can also be searched, either using the Search option from the left menu pane, or by using the voice search function.

Movie Categories

Movies are hosted on Amazon Fire TV in different categories. These categories are dependent on things like genre and availability.

Recently Added to Prime – Movies which have been recently made available for Amazon Prime Users

Shop New Release Movies – Movies which are available to buy or rent via Amazon Instant.

Recommended Movies - Movies recommended by Amazon Fire TV based on your viewing habits.

Top Movies on Prime – Movies which are the most popular among all Amazon Prime users.

Shop Top Movies - Movies for purchase or rental which are the most popular among all Amazon Instant users.

Genre Recommendations – Recommended films from various genres, based on what's popular on Amazon and your own viewing preferences.

Editor's Picks – Curated lists based on thematic similarities.

Recently Watched – Your recently viewed content.

Choosing a Movie

Once you've located a movie you'd like to watch, scroll to its thumbnail image. You will see a number of action options beneath the title thumbnail.

Watch Now means the movie will begin playing immediately.

Add to Watchlist adds the movie to your Watchlist for later viewing.

Watch Trailer will start playing the trailer for the selected movie. This option is only available for titles for purchase or rental.

Remove from Recommended Movies will remove the movie from your list of recommendations. This will also help Amazon Fire TV further hone your viewing preferences. This option is only available for recommended content.

Movie Viewing

Once you've selected a movie to watch, it should start playing automatically. You may pause the movie at any point by pressing the pause/play button. Resume play by pressing the button again. You can also use the rewind and fast-forward keys to move forward or backward in the movie.

Pressing either of these buttons once will track backwards or forwards 10 seconds. Hold down the buttons to continuously rewind or fast-forward. Pressing and holding these buttons repeatedly will advance or rewind the movie at faster speeds. You can exit the movie-viewing screen at any time by pressing either the home or back buttons.

Watching TV

As with movie content, TV shows can be accessed from the home screen one of two ways: either via the appropriate category in the left menu pane, or by scrolling through one of the thumbnail menus in the right pane of the main screen. TV content can also be searched, either using the Search option from the left menu pane, or by using the voice search function.

TV Categories

TV shows are hosted on Amazon Fire TV in different categories. These categories are dependent on things like genre and availability.

Recently Added to Prime – TV shows which have been recently made available for Amazon Prime Users

Shop Latest TV – TV shows which are available to buy or rent via Amazon Instant.

Recommended TV - TV shows recommended by Amazon Fire TV based on your viewing habits.

Your TV Shows – Content which you have already purchased via Amazon Instant appears here.

Top TV on Prime – TV series which are most popular on Amazon Prime.

Shop Top TV – TV shows for purchase or rental which are the most popular among all Amazon Instant users.

Genre Recommendations – Recommended TV shows from various genres, based on what's popular on Amazon and your own viewing preferences.

Editor's Picks – Curated lists based on thematic similarities.

Recently Watched – Your recently viewed content.

Choosing a TV Show

Once you've located a TV show you'd like to watch, scroll to its thumbnail image. To add an entire TV series to your Watchlist, select "Add to Watchlist" from beneath the series thumbnail image. To watch an individual episode, you must first select the series thumbnail, which will bring you to the TV launch page.

Watch Now will begin playing the episode immediately. This option is only available for shows that you already have the right to access via Amazon Prime.

Buy Episode selects an individual episode for purchase. The episode will begin playing immediately after you confirm your purchase. If you prefer to watch later, the episode is available to watch under Video Library at the home screen.

Buy Season purchases the whole season of the TV show and makes all episodes within that season available to watch. If you prefer to watch later, the season is available to watch under Video Library at the home screen.

Add to Watchlist adds the TV series to your Watchlist.

More Ways to Watch will reveal a menu with other viewing possibilities. TV shows may be available in different definition formats, or on different viewing platforms, including Amazon Prime.

Next Episode Available will check for the most recent available episode in a series for purchase. This option is only available with some TV series.

TV Viewing

Once you've selected a TV show to watch, it should start playing automatically. You may pause the TV show at any point by pressing the pause/play button. Resume play by pressing the button again. You can also use the rewind and fast-forward keys to move forward or backward in the show.

Pressing either of these buttons once will track backwards or forwards 10 seconds. Hold down the buttons to continuously rewind or fast-forward. Pressing and holding these buttons repeatedly will advance or rewind the TV show at faster speeds. Pressing the menu button during playback will also display the options available for the individual TV show.

These could include turning captions on or changing the language. You can exit the TV viewing screen at any time by pressing either the home or back buttons.

Playing Games On Your Amazon Fire TV

The main games page can be accessed via the left navigation pane on the home screen. Simply scroll down to "Games" and press the right navigation button to enter the main Games menu. Games are presented in four categories:

Your Games Library is where you'll find games you have already purchased or downloaded.

Popular Lists show categories of games that are popular among Amazon Fire TV users.

Spotlight presents individual games that are currently featured by Amazon.

Categories presents games divided by genre or type.

To browse games in any of the categories listed above, simply scroll to that category thumbnail using the navigation circle and press the select button. Once within a specific category, you can browse using the navigation left and right buttons.

The Amazon Fire Game Controller

Many games are compatible with, or require, the use of the Amazon Fire game controller. The game controller is sold separately, for $39.99, and is not included in your basic Amazon Fire TV pack.

Many games available via Amazon Fire TV will only function properly with the Amazon Fire game controller activated. The Amazon Fire game controller can also be used as a remote control when activated. Some third-party wireless controllers will also work with Amazon Fire TV.

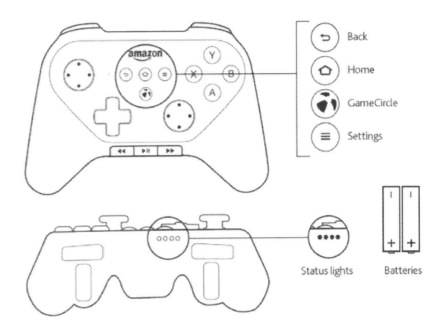

Back

Home

GameCircle

Settings

Status lights   Batteries

Using the Amazon Fire Game Controller

To begin using the Amazon Fire Game Controller, install the included AA batteries. Batteries should be installed beneath the sliding panel on the reverse side of the controller. Simply slide the cover down, install the batteries, and snap the cover back into place.

Once the batteries are installed, the controller should automatically sync with your Amazon Fire TV. If the device is not automatically detected, press and hold the home button for five seconds and then release it. This should force Amazon Fire TV to recognize the controller. Your Amazon Fire TV can be used to control both gameplay and TV and movie viewing.

Back – Returns to the previous screen.

Home – Returns to Amazon Fire's home screen from any screen.

Settings – Reveals menu information specific to whichever screen you are currently accessing.

Amazon Game Circle – Accesses the Game Circle dashboard from any screen.

Rewind – Scrolls backwards through playing media. Press the button once to jump back 10 seconds in time, or hold it down to continuously scroll backwards. Additional presses allow you to choose from various rewind times.

Play/Pause – Play or pause the current media. Press once to pause playing media, and then press gain to continue playing.

Fast Forward - Scrolls forwards through playing media. Press the button once to jump forward 10 seconds in time, or hold it down to continuously scroll forward. Additional presses allow you to choose from various fast forward times.

A, B, X, Y and Trigger Controls – Used to preform different functions within gameplay. Functions are specific to individual games.

D-Pad and Toggle Stick – Used within gameplay to perform directional functions. These buttons can also be used to navigate menus outside of gameplay.

Status Lights – Illuminate to display when the game controller is on and synced with Amazon Fire TV. Status lights also display player number when more than one controller is activated.

Purchasing and Downloading Games

Once you have paired your game controller with Amazon Fire TV (if you elect to use the game controller), you will be ready to begin browsing games. If you choose not to purchase the Amazon Fire Game Controller, you will still be able to access and play many games using your Amazon Fire Remote.

To browse games, simply select a category from the main screen and browse using the navigation circle. Once you find a game about which you would like more information, you can select the game to go to its main page. On this page, you can view game details, reviews, and similar games, as well as see screenshots and, in some cases, trailers for the game.

From the buttons on the horizontal scroll beneath the main game information, you can also look up key details, which give you additional and location-based information about the game, and see information on the game's compatibility with the Fire TV Remote or Game Controller.

On this screen you will also see the option to purchase the game. Amazon Fire TV games are commoditized in two ways. The first, in USD, is shown as a dollar amount, for example $1.99. The second is via Amazon Coins.

Amazon Coins

Amazon Coins are Amazon's unique currency, used for purchasing Games and other products via Amazon Fire TV. Amazon Coins are generally equivalent to one US cent, but are discounted by Amazon at bulk purchase amounts. For example, Amazon Fire TV may offer the possibility to purchase 500 Amazon Coins for $4.80 USD, a savings of 4%.

When you enter a game's main screen you will see the number of Amazon Coins currently in your personal bank, usually next to the "Buy" button. To purchase more Amazon Coins, scroll to the button listing the number of Coins currently in your bank and select it. A pop-up menu will show available Coin bundles and their purchase prices. To purchase one of these packages, scroll to the amount of Amazon Coins you'd like to buy and hit the select button.

Once you've found a game you would like to purchase, scroll to the purchase button and hit select. You will be prompted to choose whether or not you'd like to pay in USD or Amazon Coins. Once you choose, your game will begin downloading. If the game is "Free" simply select this button and your game will begin downloading.

Playing Games

Once the game has been downloaded, you must open it to begin playing. If you are still on the game screen, the "Buy" button will change to an "Open" button. You can select this to begin playing. Downloaded and purchased games can also be accessed from the main Games screen, under "Your Games Library."

Once within the game, your Fire Remote or Fire Game Controller will function differently, based on the individual game controls. You can still exit the game by pressing the back button, or by pressing the home or menu buttons and navigating the appropriate menus.

Amazon Fire TV games will autosave your progress, so there is no need to perform a manual save. Amazon Fire games also track your progress in individual games and save those in your GameCircle profile

Amazon GameCircle

Amazon GameCircle is a user-created profile that stores games statistics in the Amazon Cloud that can be compared with other Amazon GameCircle users. Your Amazon GameCircle profile can be displayed to track and show your game statistics.

If you have not yet set up your GameCircle profile, it will be hidden as a default. To set up the GameCircle profile, go to the main Games screen. At this screen, press the menu key. The popup menu will ask if you would like to display your profile. Press the select button again to setup your Game Circle profile.

Once you are at the GameCircle profile screen you will be prompted to fill in a nickname. This is the name GameCircle will display when assembling your statistics. Once you have selected a GameCircle nickname, you can choose a profile picture, or avatar. Once you have chosen both a nickname and a profile picture, select "Save and Continue." You should now return to the main games screen. You should notice your profile name and avatar have appeared in the top right corner.

Amazon Whispersync

Some games and apps will also sync via Amazon Whispersync. Whispersync makes sure to sync Amazon account settings across all Amazon devices logged in under the same account. All your personal account information will be saved and transmitted among your various Amazon devices so you can pick up where you left off, regardless of which device you're using.

Using Apps On Your Amazon Fire TV

Apps are programs that are installed on your Amazon Fire TV to enhance your viewing, gaming, music, and information experience. Just as in any mobile smartphone, apps can perform a wide variety of functions, ranging from the very broad to very specific. Downloading and managing apps is a great way to personalize your Amazon Fire TV experience.

As with games, apps are presented in four categories:

Your Apps Library is where you'll find apps you have already purchased or downloaded.

Popular Lists show categories of apps that are popular among Amazon Fire TV users.

Spotlight presents individual apps that are currently featured by Amazon.

Categories presents apps divided by genre or type, for example, Finance apps or Music apps.

Purchasing and Downloading Apps

As with games, apps can be browsed and then purchased for download to your Amazon Cloud. Unlike games, however, you will notice that your Amazon Fire TV comes preloaded with a number of apps, found in Your Apps Library.

These apps are ready to use, simply by scrolling to the app and pressing the select button. Some preloaded apps may require a quick download before you open them for the first time.

If you would like to remove an app from your apps library, scroll to the app and select "remove from cloud" beneath its thumbnail image. At the popup dialog, confirm that you would like to delete the app from your cloud, and it will be removed. Note that, once removed, you will lose any information you had saved in the app, including subscription information and additional content downloaded within the app.

Once you have found an app you would like to download, select its thumbnail image to go to the main app page. From this page, you will have the option to see app details, similar apps, and read app reviews. You can also view your Amazon Coin balance, see important details about the app and view screenshots or watch trailers showing the app's capabilities.

To purchase the app, scroll to the button displaying the app price, usually the leftmost in the horizontal crawl beneath the summary paragraph, and select it. You will be prompted to choose whether you'd like to pay for the app in USD or Amazon Coins (for an explanation of Amazon Coins, see Amazon Coins, in Games). The app will begin installing automatically. If the app is free, select the "Free" button and the app will begin installing.

Using Apps

Once the app has been downloaded, you must open it to begin using the app. If you are still on the app screen, the "Buy" button will change to an "Open" button. You can select this to open the app. Downloaded and purchased games can also be accessed from the main Apps screen, under "Your Apps Library."

Once within the app, your Fire Remote or Fire Game Controller will function differently, based on the individual app controls. You can still exit the app by pressing the back or home buttons at any time.

To uninstall apps from your apps library, scroll to the app thumbnail, and choose "uninstall," beneath the thumbnail. Selecting "uninstall" will remove the app, but will retain its content. To completely remove the app's contents, you must also select "remove from cloud," beneath the thumbnail image.

Viewing Photos and Personal Videos On Your Amazon Fire TV

Amazon Fire TV pulls photos and personal videos directly from media which you upload to Amazon Cloud. Amazon Cloud is an application that can be accessed via your personal computer or mobile smartphone (for more information, see Using Amazon Cloud Drive, above). Any photos or videos uploaded to your Cloud will automatically become available on your Amazon Fire TV.

The Photos page is accessed via the left navigational pane at the home screen. Scroll to Photos and press the select button. From the main photo page, you can view photos as they are grouped in albums, view all photos that have been uploaded to your Amazon Cloud, or watch videos you have uploaded.

Within the albums page, you can select individual albums by scrolling through to the album you'd like to view, then pressing select. You can also watch a slideshow of individual albums, by selecting the "Start Slideshow" button from beneath the album thumbnail.

The slideshow will automatically advance through your album. Once it has reached the end, it will return to the beginning of the photo album and start again. To scroll through the album at your own pace, press the right or left navigation buttons. Exit the slideshow by pressing the back key. You will return to the main albums page.

Albums can also be set as your Amazon Fire TV screen saver. To do so, scroll to the album you want to set as your screen saver within the albums page. Select "Set As Screen Saver," beneath its thumbnail image.

To revert to Amazon's default screen saver, please see System , below.

To view all the photos uploaded to your Amazon Cloud, select "All" from the main photo page. From the all page, you can view a slideshow of all your photos by selecting "Start Slideshow" beneath the thumbnail images of your photos. As with album slideshows, photos will advance automatically from beginning to end, and restart from the beginning.

To scroll through manually, press the left and right navigation buttons on your remote control. Press the back button to exit the slideshow and return to the all photos page.

To view the videos uploaded to your Amazon Cloud, scroll to videos and press the select button. Once within the videos page, scroll left and right to select the video you would like to watch.

To add photos & videos, you must have Amazon Cloud Drive installed on your personal computer, tablet, or smartphone. For an explanation of your Amazon Cloud Drive, see Using Amazon Cloud Drive, above.

Amazon Fire TV Settings

While it will rarely be necessary to for you to access your Amazon Fire TV's settings menu, familiarizing yourself with these options can greatly enhance your Amazon Fire TV experience, and will also help you troubleshoot problems and further personalize your Amazon Fire TV.

To access the main settings menu, scroll to the bottom of the left pane menu from your Amazon Fire TV Home screen. Once you have scrolled to "Settings" on the left pane, press either the select button or the right navigation button to enter the main settings menu.

The settings menu is organized as a horizontal crawl of different settings options. To navigate between the options, simply use the right and left navigation buttons. Press select when you have arrived at the settings option you desire to access.

Each settings option, explained below, performs a different function that will change your Amazon Fire TV user experience.

Help

The Help menu is designed to assist users in troubleshooting issues with their Amazon Fire TV unit. If you are having problems with your Amazon Fire TV, a quick trip to the Help menu may be useful in averting a lengthy exchange with Amazon customer service. Accessing the Help menu is the first recommended step when troubleshooting any Amazon Fire TV issues.

Once you have selected the Help menu, you will see a popout menu of three options: Help Videos, Quick Tips, and Contact Us. Use the up and down navigation buttons to select the option you want.

Help Videos

Help Videos are quick video tutorials that address different aspects of your Amazon Fire TV use and operation. These are designed to be easy to understand and apply, and cover a wide range of topics.

These are:
Basics (understand the basic layout of the Amazon Fire TV interface), Settings (learning to use the Settings menu), Controllers and Remotes (syncing Amazon Fire TV Remotes and Game Controllers with your Amazon Fire TV), Movies and TV (tips on watching movies and TV shows), Photos, Personal Videos and Screen Savers (tips about using the Photos menu and Amazon Cloud Drive), Games and Apps (tips on using games and apps), Troubleshooting (self-diagnosing and fixing Amazon Fire TV issues), Set Up (connecting and initializing your Amazon Fire TV), and Welcome (the Amazon Fire TV introductory video).

*You can access and rewatch these videos at any time.

Quick Tips

Quick tips are short, paragraph-length explanations about different aspects of Amazon Fire TV operation and installation. The Quick Tips menu is a good first stop when troubleshooting, as many minor Amazon Fire TV issues can be solved by following the directions supplied in these short instructions.

Contact Us

You can contact the Amazon Fire TV tech support staff via the Contact Us menu. Scroll between menu options to locate the category which most closely summarizes the issue you're having. Once you have located it, press the select button. In most cases, you will be directed to a sub-menu that more closely describes specific problems.

Once you have selected one of these issues, Amazon Fire TV will ask for your phone number. If your telephone number is already registered with Amazon, it will appear onscreen. If not, you will be prompted to enter your telephone number. If you would like Amazon to contact you via a telephone number other than the one on your Amazon account, select "Other phone number" from the menu.

Amazon Fire TV tech support can also be found online, at www.amazon.com/firetvsupport

My Account

The "My Account" menu allows you to control your personal account options as they relate to Amazon Fire TV. Here, you can check your account information and update your synced content.

Amazon Account

This menu options will display the account name currently synced with your Amazon Fire TV. If no account has yet been registered with Amazon Fire TV, you can do so here. Simply select "Amazon Account" and you will be prompted to enter your account information. If you have already registered a particular account with Amazon Fire TV and would like to unregister, you can also do that here.

Select "Amazon Account" – you will notice that the account name is displayed next to this text. Once you have selected this menu, you will be presented with the option to Deregister your account. Note that, if you deregister your account, you will lose all the Amazon Fire TV data associated with that account, and be prompted to register with a different account. Do not deregister your Amazon Fire TV unless you plan to immediately re-register with a different account name.

Sync Amazon Content

Generally speaking, Amazon content, that is, movies, TV shows, apps, games, and uploaded photos and videos, so should automatically sync with your Amazon Fire TV account when they are installed via your Amazon account or uploaded to your Amazon Cloud Drive.

If, for some reason, you notice that content is missing, you can force an immediate content sync via this option. Scroll to "Sync Amazon Content" and hit the select button. You should see the sync symbol revolve while your content is synced. Once the symbol stops moving it means that Amazon Fire TV has successfully synced with your Amazon account.

Second Screen

Amazon Second Screen is a feature that allows you to use compatible tablet devices, such as the Kindle Fire, to browse Amazon Instant and transmit this information to your Amazon Fire TV.

To use a compatible table device in concert with Amazon Fire TV, you must first ensure that both the tablet and Fire TV are connected to an online network. Amazon recommends using the same network, as this will increase efficiency and communication between the devices. Both devices must also be registered with the same Amazon account or they will not be able to communicate with one another.

To use second screen, you must also make sure that the option is activated on your Amazon Fire TV. To do so, select the Second Screen option from the Settings menu. The popout menu will show the text "Second Screen" with an On/Off option next to it. Make sure that this button is illuminated blue, and that the text reads "On." This will enable the Second Screen function on your other compatible device.

From your compatible tablet, find a movie or TV show to watch via Amazon Instant. Once you've located the video you'd like to watch, you should see a "Send To" icon on the "Watch" button. Press the "Send To" icon and then select your Amazon Fire TV from the list of available devices (it will likely be the only available device).

Once the video begins, you can use your tablet's normal video controls, such as play/pause, rewind, fast-forward, and jump back, as well as the scroll bar, to control playback on your Amazon Fire TV.

If your content is already playing on your Amazon Fire TV, you can also activate Second Screen. To do so, swipe down from the top of your compatible tablet. This should bring up your notification screen. Here, you will see information on the media currently playing on your Amazon Fire TV. You can use the play/pause and playback functions from this screen.

Applications

From this Settings menu, you can control all the options pertaining to application settings on your Amazon Fire TV. You will see general options for Amazon Application Settings, and also specific options for Installed Applications. It is worth perusing your application options to make sure you are maximizing your apps experience with Amazon Fire TV.

Amazon GameCircle Preferences

Within this menu, you can control your GameCircle and Whispersync settings. For more info on GameCircle and Whispersync, see Amazon GameCircle and Amazon Whispersync, above. To disable your GameCircle profile, scroll to "Share your GameCircle Nickname" and press select once to turn the profile off. Press select to turn it on again.

While your GameCircle profile is turned off, your game results, scores, and public nickname will not be visible on GameCircle. You will still be able to track your scores and benchmarks, but this data will not be broadcast. If you turn your GameCircle profile back on, these results will transmit again.

If you would like to disable Whispersync for Amazon Fire TV games, scroll down to "Whispersync for Games" and press select once to disable Whispersync. When Whispersync is disabled, your game information will not sync across your Amazon devices. If you re-enable Whispersync, by pressing select again, your game data will resync with all other devices connected via your Amazon account.

Amazon Appstore Settings

Within this menu you can control your Appstore settings. The Appstore is where you purchase, download, and browse for apps for your Amazon Fire TV.

Automatic Updates

To disable, or re-enable automatic updates, scroll to this setting and use the select button to toggle automatic Appstore updates On or Off. When automatic updates are on, the Appstore will automatically update all versions of your apps without requesting access to the apps.

The exception to this is apps which have changed or feature new permissions, for which you will still be prompted to approve updates. If this feature is turned off, you will be periodically prompted to manually update your apps.

External Market Links

For apps which are hosted on third-party sites, that is, sites unaffiliated with Amazon, the Appstore may open external market links for app downloading and updating purposes. To alter these settings, scroll to "External Market Links," and press the select button.

You will be redirected to a sub-menu where you can choose among three options.

The first, "Open with the Amazon Appstore" means that external links will automatically open within the Appstore, when you select an app that links to an external market site.

The second, "Don't Open," means that no links to external market sites will open within the Appstore. Practically, this means you will probably have to navigate to that app's site to install external market apps.

"Ask Before Opening" means that the Amazon Appstore will ask permission to open external market links before doing so in the Appstore. You will have the opportunity to approve or deny this request for each app with external market links.

In-App Purchases

Some apps you download will present you with the option to purchase content from within the app. In-app content can include subscriptions, game levels, or extra functionality. Toggle this option on and off by pressing the select button. When in-app purchases are disabled, you will not be able to make these kinds of purchases. Re-enabling in-app purchasing will allow you to make these sorts of purchases within the app.

Manage My Subscriptions

To manage your Amazon Appstore subscriptions, you must go online to www.amazon.com/appstoresubscriptions. Selecting this option will prompt you to visit the website.

Managing Installed Applications

Your management options will change based on the apps you have installed, and this is the place where you can manage individual app options. Scrolling to an app and selecting it will bring you to the app's info screen.

You will see some data about the app, including how much storage space it is using, and options relating to the app in the left pane. While options may vary, many apps will share some options in common, a few of which can be very useful.

Force stop can be used to quit apps that have become non-responsive or buggy. Scroll to the problematic app, select it and then scroll to "force stop" and press select. The app will quit, and should return to normal functionality when you re-open it.

Clear data will delete all the files in your app's storage. This will effectively reset the app to the state it was in when first downloaded.

Clear cache will delete files stored temporarily in the app's memory. This can include frequently accessed data that helps the app run more smoothly. If an app is slow or underperforming, clearing its cache can sometimes help. You will retain most of your personal information and should not lose any long term data.

Parental Controls

From this menu, you can toggle parental controls on and off. Parental controls require that a personal identification number (PIN) is entered before purchasing or downloading any videos, apps, or in-app items. This measure ensures that no content will be downloaded or accessed that may be inappropriate for children.

You can adjust your parental controls preferences so that a PIN is required for all purchases, only for Amazon Instant Video, or only to access or download certain types of content, e.g., games, apps, or photos.

If you set up parental controls when you first started using your Amazon Fire TV, this is a good place to quickly toggle these controls on and off. If you did not initially set up parental controls, you can do so at any time from this menu. To establish parental controls, choose a PIN (personal identification number) when prompted and specify which content you would like to control, as listed in the preceding paragraph.

If you forget your Amazon Instant PIN, you can recover or establish a new one at any time by going to www.amazon.com/PIN. There, you can change your PIN by selecting the "View/Edit PIN" option.

Controllers

From this menu, you can view information on paired Amazon Fire TV controllers, and add or pair additional controllers.

To begin, scroll to the "Controllers" option and press the select button. Then, choose which device you would like to view from the popout menu: choose either "Amazon Fire TV Remotes" to view your remote settings, or "Bluetooth Gamepads" to view game controller settings.

Amazon Fire TV Remotes

Press the select key to access the Amazon Fire TV Remotes submenu. At the next screen, you will see information about your Amazon Fire TV Remote, including its battery status, software version, and serial number. This screen is useful for garnering information about your Amazon Fire TV Remote that may be helpful for troubleshooting and tech support questions.

Add New Remote

To add another, or new, Amazon Fire TV Remote, select this option. Your Amazon Fire TV console will scan, via Bluetooth, for Fire TV Remotes within its range. When attempting to add new remotes, ensure that the batteries have been installed in the new remote, and that it is in the vicinity of the Amazon Fire TV device you would like it to control. Taking these measures will help the Fire TV console to recognize the new remote.

When you are ready to pair your new remote, select the "Add New Remote" option, then press and hold the home button on your new remote while the Amazon Fire TV device scans for the remote. The new remote should automatically pair with your Amazon Fire TV.

Bluetooth Gamepads

To add a game controller, or pair a new game controller with your existing one, select this option. From the submenu, you will see the option to "Add Bluetooth Gamepads."

To pair the new controller with your Amazon Fire TV, make sure that batteries are installed in the game controller and that it is active. If using a third-party game controller, make sure it is on the list of approved and compatible game controllers, available at www.amazon.com/tv/controllers.

When you are ready to pair your new game controller, select "Add Bluetooth Gamepads," and hold the home button on your game controller for five seconds, while your Amazon Fire TV scans for controllers. Your game controller will automatically pair with your Amazon Fire TV.

System

The system screen gives under-the-hood access to the inner
workings of your Amazon Fire TV. Here, you can calibrate
technical aspects of your Amazon Fire TV's specifications and get
device-specific data.

About

The "About" menu gives specific data about various operating
aspects of your Amazon Fire TV.

Amazon Fire TV

Scroll to this menu to see information about your Fire TV device.
Here, you can view your Fire TV device name, its storage
capacity and available storage, the synced Amazon account
name, current software version, serial number, and date and
time. Information like your serial number and software version
may be necessary to ascertain when troubleshooting, so this
screen can be useful in that event.

Network

Scroll to this menu to see information about your current
network connection, including your IP Address, Gateway,
Subtnet Mask, DNS and Mac Address.

Controllers

This menu gives you a list of connected controllers. Note that
only controllers which are currently connected to your Amazon
Fire TV will show up on this menu. To see more information
about individual controllers, press the select button. You will be
redirected to the "Controllers" menu.

Check for System Update

On this menu, you can see your current software version, the date of its installation, and the last date Amazon Fire TV checked for an update. To manually check for an update, simply scroll to "Check for System Update" and press the select button.

Screen Saver

From this menu, you can control your screen saver preferences. The screen saver will start after your Amazon Fire TV is idle for some time, and before it goes into sleep mode.

Preview

Select this option to see a preview of your screen saver. You can exit this preview at any time by pressing the back button.

Album

Scroll to this option and press select to choose which photo album you'd like to use for your Amazon Fire TV screen saver. The Fire TV comes preloaded with the Amazon Collection, and defaults to this photo album for your screen saver. However, when you select this option, you will see all other photo albums which you have uploaded to the Amazon Cloud Drive.

To select any of these albums, scroll to the option and press select. The selected album will illuminate gold, with a check mark next to it.

Shuffle

Toggle shuffle on to display screen saver photos in a random order. Screen saver defaults to playing through your photo album chronologically. When enabled, shuffle will randomly display your images.

Slide Style

Select "Slide Style" to change the way photos are displayed during the screen saver. Amazon Fire TV offers three display options:

Pan & Zoom displays photos with slow zoom ins and pans across the photo.

Dissolve fades between images in the photo stream.

Mosaic shows photos in a tiled pattern, scrolling from right to left.

Slide Speed

Select "Slide Speed" to change the transition speed between photos in your screen saver: slow, medium, or fast. This will alter the rate at which photos appear and disappear in your screen saver slideshow.

Start Time

In the start time menu, you can select the length of idle time you want Amazon Fire TV to wait before transitioning to your screen saver. Idle time is any period of time when you are not viewing or using Amazon Fire TV media, and when you are not actively engaging with the remote control or game controller.

You can stipulate an idle period of five, ten, or fifteen minutes before the screen saver engages. You can also select "never" meaning that the screen saver will not ever turn on, regardless of idle time.

Network

This menu displays your network settings and allows you to configure network settings. If you are using WiFi, you can select your WiFi network and enter you password at this screen. If you are using a wired network, Amazon Fire TV will automatically detect your network settings.

Advanced users may want to manually configure their networks. To do so, select "Network" from the Settings menu, and then select "Configure Network." You will be prompted to enter your network configuration information.

Quiet Time

Enabling quiet time will stop notifications from appearing onscreen or registering aloud. Toggling this on is a good way to ensure uninterrupted Fire TV viewing.

Collect App Usage Data

When this switch is toggled On, Amazon Fire TV will collect data about your in-app usage habits. These could include the amount of time spent using an app, the amount of data transferred and other app activity. If you would like Amazon Fire TV to stop tracking this data, toggle the switch to Off.

Developer Options

Developer options are for advanced users developing new apps and other software for the Amazon Fire TV. If you would like, you can turn off ADB debugging by press select at "Developer Options" and then toggling "ADB debugging" into the On position by pressing select again.

This will allow any user on your network to install applications on your Amazon Fire TV. While this option can be useful for developers field testing new Fire TV apps, it is not recommended for most Amazon Fire TV users.

Display

In this menu, you can set the display options to maximize your Amazon Fire TV viewing experience.

Video Resolution

In this submenu, you can change the video resolution at which Amazon Fire TV content will display. Generally, choosing "Auto" is the most effective option, as Amazon Fire TV will auto-detect your display settings and calibrate accordingly.

However, if you know your display's resolution mode and want to set it yourself, press select at "video resolution." Scroll to the appropriate setting, and then press select again to set the new video resolution.

Calibrate Display

To make sure that Amazon Fire TV is appropriately sized to your display setting, press select at "Calibrate Display." You will see a display adjustment screen, where you can use your up and down navigation buttons to center the image.

Once you have the image centered on your screen, scroll left or right to "Accept" and press the select button. To reset the display to its original setting, scroll left or right to "reset" and press the select button.

Audio

Select the "Audio" submenu to set your audio preferences.

Navigation Sounds

Navigation Sounds are sounds that play while you navigate Fire TV menus. You may toggle these on and off at this screen.

Dolby Digital Output

If you have a compatible Dolby Digital system, you can connect it via this submenu. Press select to enter the Dolby Digital menu. At this screen you will be prompted to select whether your Dolby Digital system is connected via HDMI or via the Amazon Fire TV's optical out. Scroll to the appropriate option, and press select. If you do not have a Dolby Digital compatible system, simply select "Dolby Digital Plus OFF."

Time Zone

You can set your time display preferences at the "Time Zone" menu.

24-Hour Time

Toggle this function on and off to display the time in 12 or 24-hour time. For example, 1 pm in the afternoon would display as "1:00" in 12-hour time, and "13:00" in 24-hour time.

Time Zone

Scroll to this option and press select to set your time zone preferences. Amazon Fire TV defaults to Pacific Daylight Time (PDT, UTC -7:00), so you may have to change this setting if you reside in another time zone. Scroll to your time zone and press select to reset Fire TV's clock.

Legal and Compliance

From this menu you can view legal notices and terms of use for Amazon Fire TV, generally, and also for specific functions, such as voice search. You can also view notices about safety and compliance, and terms of use. To view any of these notices, scroll to the option and press select. Your notices will appear in popup text onscreen.

Reset to Factory Defaults

To restore your Amazon Fire TV to its factory settings, select this option. You will be prompted again to make sure you want to reset your Amazon Fire TV once you have selected this option. Doing so will delete all individual settings and account settings you made to your Amazon Fire TV, and will require you to register the device again. Restoring factory defaults may be useful as a last resort in troubleshooting, but is not recommended.

Troubleshooting Your Amazon Fire TV

While the Amazon Fire TV is designed to run easily and with very little user maintenance, problems do still occasionally arise. This quick troubleshooting guide will help you remedy basic problems that may come up during routine operation of your Amazon Fire TV device.

Connection Issues

If you are unable to connect via WiFi, please note that Amazon Fire TV can only connect to particular WiFi network and modem types. Accepted modem types are B, G, and N routers on 2.4 Ghz, and A and N routers on 5 Ghz. Amazon Fire TV can only connect to encrypted networks, i.e., WEP and WPA/WPA2, both PSK and EAP.

Here are a few other steps for addressing connectivity issues:

- If your network is hidden, please follow the steps above, under Operation > Connecting to the Internet to join your hidden network.

- If you are connected to a compatible network type but still cannot access the Internet, you should ensure that your wired or wireless modem is working. Check other devices with Internet connectivity, or monitor the status lights on your modem.

- If you are connecting via WiFi, make sure wireless connectivity, found in Systems > Wi-Fi is enabled.

- If you are still having trouble connecting to your wireless network, make sure that your Amazon Fire TV is within range of your wireless hub. Please note that material obstructions, like thick walls and furniture made of thick materials, will progressively weaken your wireless signal strength.

- If you have changed settings, or are still having trouble, disconnect the power from your Amazon Fire TV for three seconds and then reconnect the unit. This sometimes helps solve communication issues between your network and Amazon Fire TV.

Controller Issues

Sometimes you may have issues getting your Amazon Fire TV to correspond with your remote or game controller. Here are a few tips for troubleshooting controller issues:

- If using a third-party controller, make sure it is compatible with your Amazon Fire TV. A list of compatible controllers can be found at www.amazon.com/tv/controllers.

- Make sure that you are attempting to control your unit from within 30 feet. Amazon controller signals are not reliable outside of 30 feet. Further, make sure that your unit is unobstructed by thick walls or furniture, as these materials could significantly weaken signal strength.

- Force Amazon Fire TV to resync with the remote. First, remove the batteries from your controller and wait a few minutes. Reinstall the batteries and allow Fire TV a few minutes to recognize your remote. If it still does not recognize the remote, hold down the home button for 5 – 10 seconds. This should force Fire TV to recognize the remote.

- If you have changed settings, or are still having trouble, disconnect the power from your Amazon Fire TV for three seconds and then reconnect the unit. This sometimes helps fix connection issues between Amazon Fire TV and your controllers.

Content Issues

If you find that you are unable to access certain or all content on your Amazon Fire TV, follow these steps:

- Make sure that you are still signed in to your Amazon account. You must have your Amazon account active and communicating with the network to access content on Amazon Fire TV.

- Ensure that you are using the correct account type. If you would like to access Amazon Prime content, make sure that you are logged in under your Amazon Prime account name, and not a different Amazon account.

- If an app, game, or media is frozen, try force stopping it and opening it again. You can find the force stop option in Settings > Applications.

Hard Reset to Factory Defaults

If you believe your Amazon Fire TV has become non-operational because of a more serious issue, you can try resetting it to factory defaults, as this sometimes will solve the problem.

Please note that, if you carry out a hard reset, you will lose all personal data entered into, or saved on, Amazon Fire TV. Data uploaded to Amazon Fire TV via Cloud Drive or your Amazon account will stay synced with your Amazon account, and will resync once you reenter your Amazon account name.

To perform a hard reset, hold the back button and right navigation button at the same time for 20 seconds, on any screen. You will be prompted with text ensuring you want to do a hard reset. Confirm that you do, and your Amazon Fire TV will reboot with factory default settings intact.

For more information on the Amazon Fire TV, or for advanced troubleshooting, please visit Amazon's Fire TV website, at: http://www.amazon.com/FireTV

Made in the USA
Lexington, KY
16 December 2015